LIFE FILES

GANGS &
BULLIES

LIFE FILES

GANGS & BULLIES

ROSEMARY STONES

Evans

EVANS BROTHERS LIMITED

Evans Brothers Limited
2A Portman Mansions
Chiltern Street
London W1U 6NR

Reprinted 2006

British Library Cataloguing in
Publication Data.

Stones, Rosemary
   Gangs & Bullies. - (Life Files)
   1.Gangs - Juvenile literature
   2.Bullying - Juvenile literature
   I.Title
   302.3'4

ISBN 0 237 51810 4 (paperback)
First published 1998
©Evans Brothers Limited 1998

ACKNOWLEDGEMENTS

Editorial: Su Swallow
Design: Tinstar Design
Production: Jenny Mulvanny

For permission to reproduce copyright material the
Author and Publishers gratefully acknowledge the
following:
Cover Lupe Cunha **page 7** Pauline Cutler, Bubbles
Photo Library **page 9** Lupe Cunha **page 11** Lupe
Cunha **page 13** Orde Eliason, Link **page 14** Jeni
Mckenzie/Mckenzie Heritage **page 15** Lupe Cunha
page 16 Peter Sylent, Bubbles Photo Library **page 17**
C. Bryan/Robert Harding Picture Library **page 19** John
Birdsall Photography **page 20** V. Miles/Robert Harding
Picture Library **page 21** Frans Rombout, Bubbles **page
22** John Birdsall Photography **page 25** Orde
Eliason/Link **page 27** Robert Francis, Robert Harding
Picture Library **page 29** Lupe Cunha **page 30** John
Birdsall Photography **page 31** Jennie
Woodcock/Bubbles **page 33** Getty Images **page 35**
Getty Images **page 37** Corbis/Everett **page 39** Pauline
Cutler, Bubbles Photo Library **page 40** Orde Eliason,
Link **page 41** Edward Parker, Hutchison Library **page
43** Lupe Cunha **page 44** Nancy Durrell McKenna, The
Hutchison Library **page 47** Daniel Lainé, Corbis **page
49** Orde Eliason, Link

CONTENTS

WHAT IS BULLYING?

Bullying is a form of aggression, a kind of behaviour that deliberately sets out to intimidate or hurt another person by causing them physical or psychological distress. It occurs when the bully is more powerful than the victim - either physically or psychologically. Bullying can take place between children, between adults and children and between adults.

Physical bullying

66 A gang of girls pick on me at school. They push me around and pull my hair. Yesterday they threw my school bag into a skip outside the school gates. I'm scared to go to the toilets in case they are in there. 99

Ruth (12)

Verbal bullying

66 They keep saying my mum is a slag and I'm dirty. The things they say feel like knives going into me. 99

Gary (14)

Psychological bullying

66 When I go into the playground, the other girls just turn their backs on me or pretend I'm not there. They've been doing this for weeks. 99

Angie (15)

Bullying can take many forms, including extortion (demanding money or goods by making threats), racism (for example, picking on people because they have a different skin colour or religion), grievous bodily harm (when someone is seriously beaten up), criminal damage (when someone's property is damaged or destroyed) and coercion (when someone is bullied into doing something they don't want to do).

Physical bullying like hair pulling can cause enormous distress.

'My dad has a newsagents and I help in the shop at the weekends. Tracy comes in and helps herself to sweets from the counter without paying. I know she'd get me if I ever told. I daren't tell my dad.' Sharon (15)

'I'm the only Asian girl in my class. The others have started calling me Paki and making fun of the things I bring to eat at dinner time.' Pria (14)

'Paul punched me in the face and broke my nose and I had bruises all down my leg. I had to go to hospital. My mum wanted to go to the police but I told her it would only make it worse. He'd get me again some other time.' Errol (16)

'We had a supply teacher who couldn't keep order. I felt sorry for her - my class gave her such a bad time. She looked as if she was going to cry sometimes. I didn't dare not join in.' Jonathan (13)

'A speaker came to lecture to the sixth form - really dull. When he finished we gave him a standing ovation. He just had to take it.' Alan (16)

'The bullying from the deputy head consisted of almost constant nasty remarks designed to destroy my confidence.' Young teacher

'At my last school I was frequently beaten up and I received death threats because I am gay. It was terrible. No one bothered to help me. Teachers just stood there and did nothing.' Christopher (14)

'My stammer gets worse when people take the mickey; there's always the odd one who does it.' Annie (11)

'When I was little I was attacked by a dog. I have a jagged scar across my lip. People at school call me "scar-face". What does it matter what you look like? It's what is underneath that counts.' Jamie (9)

We tend to think of bullying as something very obvious and straightforward - a large person attacking a smaller one - and other, more subtle forms of aggression may not be recognised as bullying at all. Sometimes people feel badly treated, unhappy or even despairing but when they report being called rude names or being pushed around or manipulated, they are told that it's 'just a bit of fun' or 'horseplay' or 'teasing' and are made to feel silly for complaining about it. Unfortunately some teachers, parents and employers find it hard to understand the more subtle and cumulative ways that many bullies go about their business.

WHO GETS BULLIED?

People may encounter bullying throughout their lives in all kinds of situations. Children are bullied in schools by fellow students or by staff; and in public places, such as on the way to and from school. Adults can be on the receiving end of bullying at work, and in institutions such as old people's homes, prisons or the armed services. Bullying may also take place in the home, where parents may bully children or elderly family members, and siblings may bully each other. There have also been cases where violent children bully their parents.

With no teachers around to stop them, some school bullies continue to torment their victims off the school premises.

> **Researchers at Sheffield University reported in 1994 that most schools have at least one teacher who bullies the pupils. Sarcastic teachers even start some of the name-calling that victims suffer.**
>
> *Times Educational Supplement* May 1997

> **In May 1996 The Professional Association of Teachers reported: 'The demands upon headteachers have increased and yet they receive very little by way of training for their demanding managerial roles. It is perhaps inevitable that some may feel insecure in their position and, in the absence of appropriate skills, resort to bullying.'**
>
> *Times Educational Supplement* May 1996

RACIST BULLYING

In a report called *Children and Racism: a Childline Study*, child victims of racist bullying describe name-calling, being punched, kicked, spat on and beaten up. The report is based on more than 1,600 callers to Childline who identified themselves as being black or belonging to an ethnic minority. Of the 430 callers who had experienced racist bullying, more than half had encountered racism within their families, had suffered racist street violence and racism at school from teachers or other school staff. Research director, Mary MacLeod said: 'It is extremely difficult to maintain a sense of self-worth against such relentless persecution as the children describe.' Some of the most upsetting cases came from rural areas where the caller was the only child from an ethnic minority in the community.

> In 1994, 20-year-old Becky Walker, who suffers from cerebral palsy, sued Derbyshire County Council for failing to protect her from psychological bullying as a schoolgirl. As a 13-year-old, Becky was bullied by three older pupils who conducted a year-long campaign of whispering and staring. She suffered from post-traumatic stress disorder and shattered confidence as a result of the experience.

IT'S ONLY TEASING

"It's only teasing! Where's your sense of humour?" is a common reaction to complaints of bullying. However, there are important differences of degree between teasing and bullying. Although a teaser, like a bully, will sometimes home in on someone's vulnerability or weakness, teasing is more usually focused on a person's particularly irritating or particularly amusing habits - such as always being late or always watching television while also listening to a Walkman. This kind of teasing usually constitutes a good-humoured rebuke that carries with it an element of enjoyment of the person's peculiarities, as well as affection for them. Teasing can also be a shared understanding between two people of their respective foibles. When someone is being teased in this benign way:

- Someone is making fun in a good-humoured way.

- If the person finds it upsetting, it's a mild feeling that soon goes away.

- Often the teaser is a good friend or family member who knows the person well and cares about him/her.

- What is said is not serious or cruelly meant. The person being teased may find it funny, too.

- Sometimes the person being teased teases the teaser. It's a two-way thing.

Sisters and brothers often tease each other and get into fights. But bullying may also occur.

People who have brothers and sisters will probably have been teased a lot at home and be used to it. People who haven't had that experience may find teasing at school upsetting at first until they have had some practice. Most of us don't like being teased unless the teaser is a trusted friend. And a sense of humour is important! However, if teasing becomes cruel and causes distress, it has slipped over the dividing line between teasing and bullying and become bullying. Also, if teasing has become one-sided, then it may have become bullying.

Question
Discuss some examples of teasing with your friends. Do you all agree on what is teasing and what is bullying?

BULLYING YOURSELF

UNDERSTANDING BULLIES

Another form of 'bullying' is self-bullying. People who do this are very hard on themselves when they don't succeed, when they make a mistake or when things don't work out as they should have. Imagine, for example, auditioning for a part in a school play but not succeeding. Are you are the kind of person who says to yourself: "You were rubbish, no wonder you didn't get it. And no one likes you anyway."?   If so, you are someone who bullies yourself. (Someone else might say: "It's very disappointing not to get a part but I did my best.   Perhaps I'll try again next term.")

People who 'bully' themselves often come from families where there is no good way of thinking about mistakes or disappointments. The attitude in families like these is, if you don't get it right first time, there is something wrong with you or it's your fault (you didn't work hard enough etc). In fact, mistakes and disappointments are an inevitable and important part of life. Mistakes are bound to happen because interesting, vital people go on experimenting and trying out new things. The mistakes people make are important because they tell you where you went wrong and how to do better next time.

People sometimes find the idea that bullies deserve understanding hard to take when bullies do such mean and horrible things to other people. But the history of violent young offenders often shows them to have been bullies before their fifth birthday and to have persisted in this behaviour throughout their school life. Bullies need sympathetic and understanding adult help so that they can be released from the pain and fear they express in their bullying behaviour and learn happier ways to get on with people.

Question
'Bullies deserve sympathy and understanding.' Do you agree?

WHO BULLIES, AND WHY?

As bullying is behaviour deliberately intended to cause distress to others, a person can only be called a bully when s/he is old enough to understand her/his own feelings and those of others. Children of around five to six years of age are capable of carrying out behaviour that is intentionally hurtful. The roots of bullying may, however, start in the early years if, say, a strong child dominates a weaker or younger one and finds that s/he enjoys it.

Younger children are not yet aware of others' feelings and may not understand the hurt they are causing.

- **Children as young as three** have been found to indulge in **rough play** which results in the perpetrator laughing at the tears of the victim. Some five-year-olds are reported as directing unprovoked aggression against other children, gripping or pulling their hair, teasing, taunting or threatening ("I'll tell the teacher"; "I won't let you come to my house").

- **Children from as young as five** onwards are reported as using **extortion** (bullying in order to acquire some desirable object, usually sweets, money or toys).

- **From the age of six name-calling** has been reported which refers to some attribute of the victim or their race (fatty; carrot top; Paki; chocolate drop etc).

- **From the age of nine intimidation**, either directly physical or threatened physical, is reported. Its purpose is often to raise the status of the bully in a group that is observing his/her behaviour. Intimidation is most often associated with boys.

- **From the age of ten, verbal bullying** which demeans the status of the victim and enhances the status of the bully is reported. This is particularly associated with girls.

The bullies' most powerful weapon is, however, the fear that they provoke in the victim. If child bullies are not helped to find other ways of dealing with their aggression or other troubling feelings, it is very possible (although not inevitable) that they will continue to bully and be aggressive in adult life.

At this young age, children quickly get over squabbles and play together happily.

WHAT MAKES A BULLY?

A range of explanations have been put forward by psychologists and others to try to understand why people bully. (It is possible that in some cases there is more than one reason for bullying behaviour and that these reasons are interrelated.)

Here are some of the possible explanations that have been put forward:

- Some younger children who use bullying tactics may not yet have achieved the level of development necessary in order to understand another person's point of view. Since they cannot empathise with the feelings of distress and hurt their actions engender, they may have genuine difficulty in understanding the impact of their bullying behaviour, seeing it, perhaps, as 'messing about'.

- Some children bully because they don't know any good ways of getting on with other people. Perhaps their parents fight when they have disagreements instead of discussing them and working them out. When children live in a family or sub-culture where violence and/or manipulation is an effective and acceptable means of getting what you want, it's not surprising that it's difficult for them to learn how to get on with others without fighting and bullying.

- Bullying behaviour often reveals great anxiety about identity and about difference. Small children have a need to find sameness in order to feel safe and secure. Once young people have established a stronger sense of their own identity they are able to manage anxiety about difference in more grown-up ways and there is no longer such a need to identify with people who are the same. There is also less need to denigrate or bully those who are 'different'.

Young people with high self-esteem can enjoy being in a group without needing to resort to bullying.

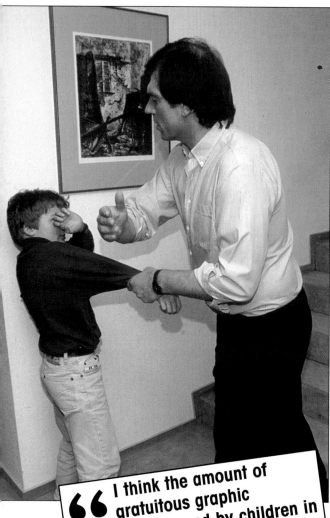

> ❝ I think the amount of gratuitous graphic violence witnessed by children in films and on television does affect their behaviour. Many experts would disagree, but common sense tells me that children learn from what they see and experience. ❞
>
> Michelle Eliot, *The Times*, August 1997

- In some cases the parents of children who are bullies use aggression to dominate other members of the household, including the children. The children may be victims of, or witnesses to, physical violence. It is not uncommon for children who are bullied at home by their parents or older siblings, to themselves use bullying behaviour at school. Hurting someone else is familiar behaviour and a way of helping themselves to feel less hurt.

- Sometimes people who are angry and upset about something and find it difficult to cope with these painful feelings will try to offload them by picking on someone else. One of the reasons that many bullies are so adept at tuning in to others' vulnerabilities is that they are so often themselves frightened and vulnerable people underneath their 'hard' front. They despise in others the weakness or fear they wish to deny in themselves. The resulting bullying is painful for the person being picked on; it is also painful for the bully not to be able to cope with difficult feelings in a better way.

- Some people bully because they are jealous or because they lack self-confidence. If they can control other people by bullying them, this helps them feel more powerful, confident and secure. They need to learn better ways to feel powerful and confident that don't involve hurting other people.

Question
Why do *you* think people bully?

TURNING A BLIND EYE

Bullying can be inadvertently encouraged by mixed messages at home from parents or at school from teachers. If children discover that 'throwing their weight around' gets them what they want, and if adults collude with this behaviour by turning a blind eye, bullying behaviour will become entrenched as both bullies and their victims come to believe that these adults find bullying acceptable.

Some children are brought up in run-down and disadvantaged communities where there is an atmosphere of violence and where law and order cannot be relied on. Their experience may be that aggressive behaviour pays off as people need to 'stand up for themselves'. Bullying behaviour may also be positively encouraged by their parents and their peers for whom being a good fighter, having 'street cred' or being the toughest guy on the block brings kudos.

Children who are victims of physical violence may themselves become bullies.

Some parents and teachers still believe that bullying is 'normal', part of life's 'hard knocks' and the only way for children to learn to cope with bullying is to be 'toughened up' by experiencing it. This attitude is prevalent in very different levels of society, from public schools where bullies may come from highly privileged backgrounds, to state schools with children from poor communities with high levels of unemployment.

DIFFERENCES BETWEEN GIRL AND BOY BULLIES

Both girl and boy bullies use the same techniques but overall, girls tend to use physical violence less frequently, preferring verbal or psychological bullying. Some researchers suggest that boys tend to seek power and dominance from bullying. Girls tend to seek to affirm a feeling of belonging and shared intimacy by excluding someone from their charmed circle, refusing to speak to their victim or saying malicious things to prove her unworthiness to be part of the group. However, there are signs that physical attacks by girls on other girls, sometimes quite vicious, are on the increase.

Find out!
What are the regulations relating to violence on the television?

Question
Do you think that screen violence encourages bullying?

WHO GETS BULLIED?

Almost everyone is bullied at some point in their school career and almost everyone will encounter bullying behaviour in their adult life. For some people it can be an unpleasant but brief episode; for others it can be a longterm nightmare of persecution.

Some happy, confident people are bullied simply because they have the misfortune to be in the wrong place at the wrong time. For them, the bullying may be an isolated incident. People who suffer sustained bullying can become victims for various reasons, but two of the main causes are difficulties about identity and difference.

IDENTITY AND DIFFERENCE

Children go through a stage of classifying people into simple groups of those like and unlike themselves and they may display hostility to those they see as different. All kinds of differences can lead to a person being bullied: red hair, a stammer, a different accent, famous parents, poor parents and so forth. Bullies also pick on victims who are seen as disadvantaged in some way - perhaps by appearance or by poverty. Children at puberty are often self-conscious about how their bodies are changing and developing. Bullying that draws attention to differences in physical development can be particularly wounding.

Being 'different' in some way from the rest of the group may lead to bullying or being bullied.

Race classification is perhaps one of the most obvious examples of bullying arising out of difference. The people who receive the most labelling in society, and in some areas the most hostility, are those who can be identified by their colour as different from the majority.

Thirteen-year-old Mancunian, Vijay Singh, wanted to be a footballer. One Saturday in 1996 his family came home to find Vijay dead. He had committed suicide. His devastated mother looked through his schoolbag for explanations and found a journal. Its last entry read:

> **"** I shall remember this for all eternity. Monday: my money is taken. Tuesday: names are called. Wednesday: my uniform is torn. Thursday: my body is pouring with blood. Friday: It's ended. Saturday: freedom. **"**
>
> *The Guardian* October 1996

Most people as they develop and grow in confidence come to understand that such classifications of difference (for example people from our street, people from outside our street, black people, white people, old people, young people, gay people, straight people, working class people, middle class people etc) are not very useful or important. They come to understand that everyone has much in common with people from other groups and also that there are differences within a group.

For some people, however, such maturity of insight can be more difficult. They may be so emotionally disadvantaged or have such limited horizons that they continue to invest in rigid and hostile notions about other groups. In the sectors of society to which they may belong, there may also be an implicit consensus about the status of various groups in the pecking order.

PICKING ON THE VULNERABLE

People with low self-esteem - that is, a poor opinion of their own worth - and people who are feeling distressed and vulnerable are often singled out by bullies. Their lack of self-confidence or level of distress may mean that they cannot defend themselves from being controlled or trampled on by other people. Bullies can be very quick to tune in to such weakness.

Sometimes a person who has been seen to be bullied is then allocated a victim role by the class or group and random bullying continues. Once such a person has been identified as vulnerable, it can be very hard to overcome the "victim" status. They may also lose support from their friends who don't want to side with a victim for fear of being bullied themselves.

It's hard to defend yourself from being hurt by others if you have a low opinion of your own worth.

Question
'If you get bullied, you should deal with it on your own.' Do you agree?

Clumsiness, whether to do with physical coordination or with social skills, can provoke bullying if the clumsy child lacks self-confidence. Children with poor coordination who are not good at games, or children who want to be friends but don't know how to join a group can find themselves isolated. Often they seek comfort in non-social activities such as computers or books, where they run no risks of being taunted or rejected. This may be a sensible short-term solution to a miserable situation, but friendship skills or good ways of dealing with reactions to physical difficulties cannot then be tested out and confidence developed.

Students who are bullied at breaktimes sometimes take refuge in the school library or computer room. But avoiding the problem may lead to further social isolation.

> **A 14-year-old girl was beaten and stamped on in the changing rooms after she had won three races at Bowling Community College sports day. Nicola Bowden found her clothes dumped in the lavatory; she was then set upon by a 14-year-old girl who held her down while the attacker's 11-year-old sister kicked and stamped on her. She was taken to Bradford Royal Infirmary with a fractured rib, internal bleeding and torn tissues in her lungs. She is now frightened to return to school.**

The Times July 1997

THE IMPACT OF BULLYING

Bullying is certainly something that is persistent and commonplace in life and of course children must learn to deal with it. Some do manage to deal with it on their own without being too hurt by it - generally they

Victims of persistent bullying may feel ashamed that they cannot find a way to stop the bullies.

are people with high self-esteem who do not allow bullying to influence how they see themselves.

Other people whose self-esteem is more fragile can find bullying so distressing that they lose confidence in themselves; their development can be stunted because they now fear social interaction with their peers. If they have been subjected to a number of attacks over a prolonged period they may also be suffering from feelings of degradation, humiliation and shame. They may even begin to believe that the abusive

names they have been called or the vicious things that have been said about them must be true - perhaps they really are unworthy and dislikeable. They may also be feeling shame that they have been unable to prevent the bullying taking place.

So far from teaching them to cope with 'hard knocks', the experience of being bullied can encourage some people to develop avoidance behaviours (keeping a low profile, dropping out of school/work, etc). Some can even suffer from depression and, in some cases, commit suicide.

All this amounts to very good reasons for people who are bullied to be afforded sensitive intervention and good strategies to deal with the problem.

However 'normal' bullying is, it is not 'normal' for people - adults or children - to live in an atmosphere of fear and insecurity, which is what happens when bullying is allowed to go on. It has been found that children who have witnessed bullying can be deeply affected by the fear that it may happen to them.

despairing about your situation and have no one to turn to, you should phone the Helplines listed at the end of this book and talk to one of their experienced and understanding counsellors.

> **In 1992 16-year-old Katherine Bamber was founded hanged in the garage of her home. In her suicide note she wrote: "I hate my life... People like —— make it hell. I hate them for threatening me and calling me a tart and a slag. I can't take it any more. I'm very scared and hurt inside by them and the only way I know out is by killing myself."**

SEEKING HELP

Suicide is an act in which intense feelings find expression in a way that is self destructive. Together with other interrelated factors, bullying can be a factor that might lead a young person to take his/her own life. Some young people who have committed suicide have left letters expressing their despair about being the victims of bullying, their feeling that nothing can be done and that life is no longer worthwhile. If you feel

ADULTS BULLYING ADULTS

One of the first studies of adults bullying adults was conducted for a BBC radio programme. There was a huge public response and the study was later published. The study demonstrated that bullying in the workplace is widespread. Many courageous women and men from all walks of life (including bank workers, civil servants, chefs, nurses, advertising executives, college lecturers and teachers) contributed their experiences of being bullied and of bullying:

> **" If the boss thought someone was doing a better job than him, he'd move them out into a cramped office that was well away from everybody else. "**
>
> Joe, an advertising executive

> **" If you challenged the boss, he would pick on you for the rest of the week, calling you offensive names in front of the others. "**
>
> Rosemary, a bank clerk

A co-author of the report, a psychotherapist, comments that 'To some bullies, the idea of a stable environment - either at work, or in ordinary human relations - would be untenable...People with whom they work can be drawn into this unhealthy environment and unwittingly forced to play a role in it.'

Bullying in the workplace is now an issue that concerns unions and many professional organisations. In a survey conducted in 1995, for example, the National Association of Schoolmasters Union of Women Teachers found that three quarters of respondents had either been subjected to serious bullying themselves or witnessed the bullying of others.

Some adults also encounter the kind of bullying that children experience at school - they are those trapped by circumstances in situations where they are powerless, in institutions or in violent relationships. These adults need protection and support as much as children and young people in schools. Frequently adults stay in jobs where they are bullied because of the fear of unemployment.

> **" I was desperate to escape from the post of deputy head in a primary school. From the start the new head set about undermining my self-confidence and became so aggressive I became afraid he might physically attack me one day. "**
>
> Teacher, *Times Educational Supplement*
> June 1995

Children who bully and children who are bullied may continue to interact with others in similar ways as adults if they are not helped to think about themselves in better ways and change their behaviour. That's a sad and unhappy way to lead a life.

When the Trades Union Congress (TUC) set up a 'bad bosses' hotline recently, it was inundated with calls from people in all kinds of occupations who complained of bullying and exploitation.

How should adults deal with bullying at work? Some people advise victims to try to resolve problems of bullying in the workplace by confronting the bully. They recommend assertive (rather than aggressive) behaviour and suggest that bullies are weak characters who will usually back down. Others disagree, and point out that the bully is often the victim's boss, and that confronting the boss is unlikely to improve the situation. Sometimes, the personnel department or trade union can help. A few companies have an anti-bullying policy. If all else fails the victim may have to consider taking legal action.

Find out!
Find out whether large companies in your area have an anti-bullying policy.

Find out!
Look for newspaper articles about incidents of bullying in the workplace. From what you read, do the victims' complaints seem reasonable? Were the problems resolved in the best way?

66 In a recent survey, the Institute of Personnel and Development found that one in eight people had been bullied at work in the last five years. Nationally, that's three million people. 99

HOW WIDESPREAD IS BULLYING?

A HELPLINE IN JAPAN

Research into bullying began in the 1970s in Scandinavia. A Swedish physician, Peter Paul Heinemann, first drew attention to the problem after observing bullying in the playground on routine visits to schools. Large-scale and long-term academic research was then carried out in Norway, and in the 1980s the Norwegian Ministry of Education launched a nationwide campaign against bullying in schools.

Japan was the next country to take an interest in bullying at a national level. A survey was conducted and the police organised a telephone helpline for parents

Bullying was identified as a serious problem in schools in Japan following a number of student suicides.

and children. An anti-bullying panel was set up at the end of 1994 after a series of suicides of junior and senior school pupils who had been physically and mentally tormented by their classmates. In one case a 13-year-old school pupil hanged himself after bullies repeatedly extorted money from him. Another victim was unable to cope with the taunts of his classmates and jumped in front of a moving train.

The *Japan Times* reported another suicide. "I don't want to die, but going on like this is a living hell." Hirofumi Shikagawa, 13, left this note before hanging himself in a bathroom in 1986. Shikagawa's note ended with the plea: "Please stop such stupid things now. This is my last request." Shockingly, a few months before the suicide, a group of students had staged a mock funeral for Shikagawa and given him farewell messages from classmates and a few teachers. A journalist used his magazine column to urge the victims of bullying not to kill themselves, so that Shikagawa's death would not be in vain. He encouraged victims to stop going to school if they couldn't take the abuse any longer.

Takayoshi Inoue, a government minister in Japan said: 'We are seriously concerned about the growing cases of young people who suffer from bullying to the point that they commit suicide.' The Japanese Education Ministry has called on a panel of experts to analyse bullying cases to discover common causes. Based on their study, the ministry plans to come up with a comprehensive plan to fight bullying. In the meantime, the ministry, for the first time, has called on the community to involve itself in fighting this issue.

BULLYING IN BRITAIN

One of the first surveys of bullying in Britain was carried out by Michele Elliott, director of the national child-safety organisation, Kidscape. Four thousand children were studied between 1984 and 1986. More than one third claimed to have been bullied.

> " I would say that bullying is on the increase and that it is becoming nastier and more violent. "
>
> Michele Elliott,
> *101 Ways To Deal With Bullying*

One of the problems faced by researchers was that bullying can be a terrifying experience which leaves its victims too ashamed or frightened to talk about it. In addition, children who bully were understandably reluctant to admit to such behaviour. However, the suicides of a number of schoolchildren lead to greater public awareness of the problem and a greater willingness to speak out about it. In 1985, 13-year-old Mark Perry cycled into the path of an oncoming van after being continually harassed by a group of boys. His death, and that of Katherine Bamber who hanged herself after being bullied at school (see page 23), highlighted the tragic results of bullying behaviour.

STRATEGIES IN SCHOOLS

In March 1989, the Elton Report on Discipline in Schools identified bullying as 'a problem that is widespread and tends to be ignored by teachers'. The report went on to recommend that "headteachers and staff be alert to signs of bullying; deal firmly with all such behaviour, and take action based on clear rules which are backed by appropriate sanctions and systems to protect and support victims".

Despite such a clear statement and recommendations, it took almost two years before the Department for Education commissioned a research project into bullying to 'help us gain a better picture of what the situation actually is, but also to see which strategies work best to deal with the problem of bullying.' The project surveyed 25 Sheffield schools (17 junior/middle, seven secondary and one special unit). It found that as many as one in five children in those schools had been subjected to bullying.

In 1993 the annual report of Her Majesty's Chief Inspector of Schools, Professor Stewart Sutherland, stated that schools needed to tackle bullying. Professor Sutherland found that most secondary schools were affected and inspectors had seen isolated incidents of scuffles in classrooms. Nearly all schools attempt to eradicate it, he continued, but not all are successful.

Research indicates that one in four students experience bullying in schools in the UK.

Helplines receive thousands of calls a year from the victims of bullying.

CHILDLINE SURVEY

Childline is a 24-hour national telephone helpline for children in trouble or danger. Childline estimates that it counsels around 5,000 children who are being bullied each year. A temporary Childline hotline on bullying in 1990 received more than 2,000 calls in three months.

In 1996 Childline researchers conducted a survey of bullying in schools and found that 'bullying in schools is commonplace, even in schools with anti-bullying policies in place.' Sixty-four per cent of primary school children and forty-five per cent of secondary children said they had been bullied at some point in their schools. Half of the primary school children and more than one in four of the secondary children responding said they had been bullied in the last year. The survey found that boys and girls were equally represented in the primary group but that more girls than boys in secondary school said they had been bullied in the last year.

These figures include children who said they had been bullied for only a short time, perhaps a few days. If these children had been excluded, the figures for children who had been bullied would have been twenty-five per cent of primary school children and thirteen per cent of secondary children. However, Childline felt that to exclude one-off episodes of bullying or short bursts of bullying (which many children reported as causing them great fear) from their survey would be to misrepresent children's experience of bullying.

Children were also asked if they had bullied others the previous year. Eighteen per cent of primary and twenty-five per cent of secondary pupils said yes, they had. As children who bully are often reluctant to admit to such behaviour, it is likely that these figures do not reflect the true level of bullying.

Excluding someone from the group can be a powerful form of bullying.

About half of the children who had been bullied said the bullying had lasted a few days. This finding contrasted sharply with the figures for children who actually phoned the Childline Bullying Line. About half of these children said they had been bullied for over a month and up to a year. Clearly, children who called the Bullying Line were those in greater difficulty and those less able to get effective help in their schools.

A GLOBAL PROBLEM

Researchers in Australia in 1994 estimated that one child in seven was being bullied at least once a week by others. In some schools the figure was one in four. 'Many of our children live in a permanent state of anxiety because of bullying,' said Professor Ken Rigby, of the University of South Australia. 'Often, however, they dare not tell their parents or teachers what is happening.' With a colleague, Professor Rigby carried out the largest survey of school bullying undertaken in Australia. They found that half a million pupils suffer at the hands of school bullies each week.

In Seville, in Spain, in 1997 researchers found that a quarter of pupils in primary and secondary schools have experienced bullying. They found that 'pupils who suffer this violence grow up insecure, frightened and anxious while bullies become people who believe that rules are not to be obeyed. Without strategies to challenge such anti-social behaviour, these children are also at risk.'

In a survey on bullying in Portuguese middle schools in 1997, one in five children were bullied at least three or more times during the school term. Unusually, more victims were boys than girls but more victims were from low socio-economic backgrounds.

Question

A 20-year-old stockbroker accepted £30,000 damages from Richmond Borough Council to settle his claims that between the ages of 12 and 15 he was bullied at school. Do you think local authorities should compensate victims of bullying at school?

Find out!

Talk to older relatives abut bullying in their schooldays. Is there more bullying today? Is there more violence?

> **"** Police and members of the education authorities in Sandwell, near Birmingham, held an emergency meeting after the death of shy Stephen Worrall, who was found hanging from banisters at home by his seven-year-old sister, Emma. Stephen had said he hated school and was being picked on by 14- and 15-year-old boys who stole his lunch money and called his dad names. Stephen's father had written to complain that his son was being bullied. **"**
>
> *Times Educational Supplement,*
> *March 1993*

GANGS AND BULLIES IN HISTORY

ROWDY ROMANS

Like other shocking areas of human behaviour such as child abuse or domestic violence, bullying and violent gang behaviour are not new phenomena.

Ancient Rome witnessed gang behaviour more than 2000 years ago.

There is evidence, for example, in Roman history of rowdy youths in gangs beating up passers-by in the streets. Two poor men, Lucius and his brother Volscius, on their way home through the streets of Rome in 461BC, met a revelling and drunken gang: 'At first they laughed at us and abused us, as young men when drunk and arrogant are apt to abuse the humble and poor'. Lucius unwisely tried to stand up to the gang, who beat him senseless. When Volscius tried to help his brother, the same thing happened to him. Lucius later died from the effects of the beating while Volscius only just pulled through.

GANGS IN HISTORY

In Ancient Greece students as young as fifteen took part in gang warfare. Libanius, later a teacher, tells us that on his arrival in Athens as a student he was captured by one student gang only to be abducted by another who incarcerated him in a cell no bigger than a barrel.

Thomas Platter, a Swiss born in 1499, was a member of one of the gangs of young people who travelled from place to place looking for education. The oldest pupil was the leader who exploited and sometimes beat the younger members of the gang but at the same time protected and defended them from the hazards of the road and of foreign life.

Schoolboys in seventeenth-century France organised a brawl which turned into an armed riot, after being beaten in public by a master.

Valerie Besag in *Bullies and Victims in Schools* tells us that 'school logbooks dating back to the last century showed that violent attacks on pupils and teachers were not uncommon at the time'. In Manchester in the years around and during the First World War, a local Jewish vigilante gang had to be formed to protect Jewish girls and women from assault by the vicious Napoo Gang who would creep up behind them and cut off their long plaited hair.

Children and young people's involvement in gangs often depended, as it still does, on their economic circumstances. In England in the earlier part of the 20th century, many children formed gangs with strong tribal loyalties. These were strongest in working class areas and among street urchins, and their loyalty was often to the children of the street in which they lived.

Doris Bailey, born in 1916, was brought up in London's East End. Interviewed in *A Century of Childhood*, she says 'Our street, being a cul-de-sac, was a favourite place for games, and there were often fights when our own gangs turned on those from neighbouring streets and told them to get back where they belonged. The Cockney fellow's street was his kingdom, and not lightly trampled on by outsiders.'

Published in 1857, *Tom Brown's Schooldays*, a novel about Rugby School, has a famous bully, Flashman, who tyrannises the younger boys. Eventually Tom, and his friend East, come to blows with Flashman with the result that he 'never laid a finger on either of them again'. The novel contains many other instances of bullying. Tom advises a new boy, Arthur, on how best to protect himself from it: 'You must answer straight up when the fellows speak to you and don't be afraid. If you're afraid, you'll get bullied. And don't say you can sing and don't you ever talk about home, or your mother or sisters...or they'll call you home-sick, or mamma's darling, or some such stuff.'

Question
What advice would a modern-day Tom give to a new boy? Would a girl's advice to a new girl be the same? What would your advice to a new pupil be?

Street gangs were common in cities early in the century, but not all were threatening.

> **❝ Ray Rochford, brought up in Salford in the inter-war years, remembers: "You had to be in a gang or you were nobody. And every so often, the word would go round that a gang from another street or another neighbourhood was coming round for a fight. Everyone armed themselves with sticks and stones and bricks. It was mostly the boys but you'd get a few girls there in the front line. Most of them, though, were weapon carriers. You wouldn't believe the violence, it was like the Battle of Crecy. There was bricks flying everywhere, broken glass, fists flying. I was terrified but you daren't show it; if you showed yourself to be a coward your life wasn't worth living - you'd be shunned. ❞**
>
> *A Century of Childhood*
> by Steve Humphies, Joanna Mack and Robert Perks,
> Channel 4 Books

Not that bullying in public schools seems to have changed much in the course of the twentieth century. Writer Roald Dahl never forgot being caned by a bullying headmaster at his prep school and later being bullied by the boy whose study he had to clean. 'All through my school life I was appalled by the fact that masters and senior boys were allowed literally to wound other boys, and sometimes quite severely...At the end of (one beating), a basin, a sponge and a small clean towel were produced by the headmaster, and the victim told to wash away the blood before pulling up his trousers.'

In his biography *Prince Charles, The Prince of Wales*, Jonathan Dimbleby describes how Prince Charles was bullied at Gordonstoun because he is heir to the throne.

> **❝ Novelist Jilly Cooper was at a girls' public school, Godolphin School, Salisbury: 'We bullied Jennifer because she was fat and Enid because she had large breasts at 11. It was not considered right to be so over-endowed. Our worst bullying, however, was reserved for our under-housemistress, Miss Harris. We cornered her and stripped off her clothes down to her petticoat. As a punishment we were denied sandwiches at tea.' ❞**
>
> Jilly Cooper, novelist, in *Me and My Bully*,
> article in *Evening Standard* 1994

> **Explorer Sir Ranulph Fiennes went to public school. In *Living Dangerously* he writes: 'I was full of self-assurance when I first went to Eton. Public school and three long years of remorseless nastiness squeezed every last trace of confidence from me.'**

In 1954 the writer William Golding published his best known novel, *Lord of the Flies*, the story of a party of schoolboys, survivors of a plane crash who have to cope with being on a desert island. The boys' attempts, lead by Ralph and Piggy, to set up a democratic group soon fail and terror rules as Jack takes over as leader, ostracising those who

Fat and with spectacles, Piggy in William Golding's novel *Lord of the Flies*, becomes the first victim of bullying by the gang which some of the boys who have survived a plane crash on a desert island set up. This powerful novel was made into a film.

will not join him. Two boys are killed and it
is only with the arrival of a shocked rescue
officer that civilisation returns. Golding's
novel raises profound questions about
human nature and group behaviour and is
extensively studied in schools.

Find out!

**How is the issue of bullying dealt with in
television soaps? Do such programmes
offer any solutions?**

In the 1990s, the issue of bullying became a
topic that inspired many writers for children
and young people. Some of their titles are
listed at the back of this book.

WHY DO PEOPLE JOIN GANGS?

People are primates, members of the animal world, and like other animals they sometimes use aggression to establish a hierarchy of dominance. In primary school, young children can be seen forming themselves in gangs and establishing initiation rites, rituals and codes of conduct to distinguish themselves from those outside the gang. The dominant positions in the gang are occupied by the tougher or the more popular children.

> **When we were little we went to Wales with another family for a holiday. My sister started the Mud Gang. To become a member you had to roll in mud. I refused but the other children did it.**
>
> Fred, now 15

> **We had a password and we made badges to wear. We left each other messages at secret drops and we spied on people.**
>
> Thomas, now 17

THE PROS AND CONS

Boys tend to form gangs with a hierarchical structure in which some members dominate others, while girls tend to stress intimacy and sharing. Girls' (usually smaller) gangs seek to sustain friendships and closeness via confidences and gossip. This pattern is now beginning to change with more girls becoming involved in aggressive and dominating gang behaviour.

Girl gangs may use physical violence as well as more subtle forms of bullying such as social exclusion.

Younger children often use the gang experience in positive ways to learn what it means to be part of a team. Membership also gives opportunities to learn how to get along with others as well as to learn about solidarity, trust and judgement. Pranks and schemes may be carried out in an exciting atmosphere of conspiracy and companionship. On the debit side, as young people get older, gang rules can inhibit individual expression and members may feel obliged to modify their private selves in order to fit in.

Like football clubs, some gangs have a dress code - members are expected to wear a particular sort of clothing which identifies them as 'one of the gang'.

A PASSING PHASE

Most young people, as they grow older and develop a confident sense of their own identity, find that they no longer need or want to be a part of a gang. It's a passing phase. Instead they meet social needs by forming a group of friends and/or they join a club to share an activity (for example, a rugby team, a chess club). They no longer need the back-up a gang can provide in difficult circumstances. They are able to sort out arguments and conflicts by discussion and tolerate differences and disagreements without feeling undermined.

For these street children in Brazil, gang membership is a way of trying to survive.

AN EXTENDED FAMILY

While membership of a gang can be an enjoyable and short-term part of growing up for young people in secure circumstances, it can provide a much needed sense of structure and of belonging for other children and young people who lack adequate affection, care and stability in their home life. In these circumstances, a gang can become a kind of extended family. An extreme example of gangs serving this function can be seen in parts of Latin America and in the major cities of South Africa, where homeless and abandoned street children attempt to survive by forming themselves into gangs.

Of course, many young people do not become members of gangs at all. They may be part of a group of friends, be a 'loner' or have interests or experiences which set them apart.

Question
When does a group become a gang? Are all gangs threatening?

HIGH SPIRITS OR HOOLIGANISM?

While teenage rebellion against authority is a normal part of the process that adolescents go through in order to achieve independence and maturity, such rebellion sometimes includes the testing out of destructive wishes or the taking out of frustrations on random and innocent targets. The potential for chaotic and destructive behaviour can be high in a teenage gang if some members have such an agenda - from debagging victims at parties to throwing bottles at football matches, and from streaking to joy-riding.

Society often has an ambivalent attitude to such behaviour - public school boys and students at Oxford and Cambridge are sometimes permitted to get away with gang behaviours seen as 'high spirits' which, in less privileged young people, are condemned as 'criminal' or 'hooligan'.

Question
What is the difference between high spirits and hooliganism?

GANG BULLYING

When bullying is carried out by a gang rather than by one individual, the level of cruelty and violence used against the victim often increases, as those taking part in this group situation do not feel personally responsible for what is happening. In fact, even though they are not acting alone, each and every member of the gang involved is personally responsible for what takes place (even if they are onlookers rather than participants). However, because so many others are also taking part, there is often an assumption that the blame is 'shared' and therefore less serious; also that any punishment is likely to be more diffuse.

> 66 Katherine took an overdose three months after being set upon by an all-girl gang who had harassed her before. She suffered a 15-minute beating in front of 25 bystanders who failed to intervene. A telephone call on the evening she killed herself is said to have warned her of more troubles ahead. In suicide notes to her parents and a school friend she said that persistent bullying had made her life miserable and complained she was depressed, particularly by the effect the hostility was having on her schoolwork. 99
>
> *The Guardian* June 1997

ANIMAL AGGRESSION

Many young people who find themselves behaving badly or cruelly as part of a gang would not behave in this way if they were on their own. Their need to be part of the gang and their fear of being different to the other members lead them to avoid taking responsibility for their actions. Later, they may regret or feel ashamed about what they have done.

Another aspect of gang behaviour is the need of some bullies for an audience. Sometimes gangs include bullies who enjoy being surrounded by an appreciative crowd as they use words to torment a victim or as they use physical violence. In this situation, the level of cruelty or violence can increase because there is an audience to play to. Gang members may literally vie with each other to 'put the boot in'.

Amongst animals other than humans, there is little evidence that the different species (other than some rodents) use aggression against their own members unless such violence is needed to serve a definite function - a newly dominant male lion, for example, may kill the cubs of the previous dominant male in order to establish the supremacy of his own genes. Domestic animals of the same species may attack each other if food or space is inadequate. However, no animal attacks, torments or destroys members of its own species to the extent that humans do. Like war, forms of aggression such as bullying and gang violence serve no useful function in the preservation of the human race and are uniquely human behaviours.

When there is a playground fight, a crowd will quickly gather, providing an audience for those bullies who have a need to show off by tormenting others in public.

GANGS AND CRIME

THE IMPACT OF UNEMPLOYMENT

Many people associate crime with youth gangs but not all youth gangs are delinquent and not all gangs are made up of criminal offenders. In fact most juvenile crime is carried out by individuals or pairs. However, the violent aspect of juvenile crime committed by gangs is increasing, with knives and even guns being used. There have also been instances of sexual attacks and rapes.

In the East End of London, when racial attacks against the Asian community escalated in the 1980s, Asian youths got together to set up defence groups. In recent years with the spread of drug-dealing, more and more gangs have become involved in crime and violence, including those apeing the Chinese triads and the West Indian yardies (criminal gangs). In 1996 London headmaster Philip Lawrence was knifed through the heart when he went to help a pupil attacked by a triad-style gang outside his school. In 1997 the leader of a schoolboy gang which based itself on the Chinese triads was found guilty of murdering another boy with a machete outside their school gates. The murder was believed to be in revenge for a slight the gang had received the previous week.

In areas of high male unemployment, boys predominate in gangs, often taking part in 'fighting' behaviour - teasing and provoking each other and acting out images of violence and war. Some researchers believe that such adolescent boys feel deeply confused about their future role in society. Growing up in communities where the old dichotomy between the male breadwinner and the

Young men in areas of high male unemployment may feel that their masculinity is threatened and join gangs or become involved in fights as a way of reasserting themselves.

female home-maker has vanished, they feel threatened by their own traditional notions of maleness and may be acting out their confusions about domination and control via play-fighting and via gang warfare. Such boys find themselves in a situation where girls are now more likely to be able to find work after school than they are.

A headteacher of a primary school in Jarrow, an area where male unemployment stands at more than twenty per cent, said he was witnessing a sense of hopelessness among a small minority of young children. Ten and eleven-year-olds were beginning to believe 'with some justification' that they were not going to get a job and that 'real ambitions are just dreams'. He said: 'It is better to be famous for being a clown or a toughie than working hard and being a failure. Everyone wants a place in life, but many male adults in the area can only be important by being anti-authoritarian. These role models are set up because adults are so disaffected.'

SAFETY IN NUMBERS

Some young people join gangs because they are afraid not to - in poor urban areas many young people feel that the only way to keep safe or to feel that they are 'somebody' is to be in a gang.

> " I've just moved schools recently and I'm having a terrible time with a gang of girls in my class. They call me "tart" and "bitch" every day. Other girls in the class keep away from me because they don't want to get picked on by this gang. I feel so alone. I've told a teacher who ticked them off, but it didn't make any difference. My teacher says I need to stick up for myself, but how can I against so many? "
>
> Louise, aged 15, in a letter to *The Sun* June 1995

> " A teenage gang is alleged to have used blackmail and beatings in an eight-month reign of terror inflicted on around twenty children aged 12 and 13 at a school in Doncaster. They lay in wait outside the school and forced their victims to hand over dinner money. Ten boys aged 12 to 15 were charged with a total of 35 offences, including blackmail, robbery, assault and affray. "

GANG CHARACTERISTICS

Research into gangs in the US shows that gang members often share common characteristics. They may be victims of child abuse; many have never seen a conflict settled without the use of violence; many are school drop-outs; they have inadequate family lives. Poor and ethnic minority neighbourhoods have more gangs than middle-class neighbourhoods. Boys join gangs more often than girls do, although some girls have their own gangs and others are a part of mostly male gangs. Most gang members are older teens but not always. In Chicago, police have reported gang members as young as nine or ten years old.

The CRIPS gang in Los Angeles, USA, is one of many in that city where levels of gang violence are high in poor neighbourhoods.

RAP TO THE RESCUE

In 1988, a US rap star, KRS-One, asked a group of artists to join him in making a record called 'Self-Destruction' which aimed to encourage young people to find ways of solving problems without resorting to violence. This initiative was prompted by a high level of gang violence amongst the youths who came to see rap concerts. In 1991, in Los Angeles, rap groups got together and gave a concert just for gang members at which gang violence and the need to prevent it was discussed.

Sometimes gang opinion itself can work positively to stop bullying if the values or rules of a particular gang are against bullying behaviour. When no kudos or status is attached to bullying and there is a risk of peer disapproval, a bully will desist. A gang may also allow timid or vulnerable children to join, people who would be prime targets for attack if not protected by their gang membership.

GANG VIOLENCE IN PARIS SCHOOLS

In 1993 teachers from four secondary schools in a tough northern suburb of Paris went on strike to protest at the education ministry's inadequate response to escalating violence. Teachers in one school had been subjected to aggression by a gang of masked outsiders who burst into their classrooms - these were usually former pupils who had been sent to another school because of bad behaviour. Teachers working in Seine-Saint-Denis had been punched, threatened with knives and one was even sprayed with tear gas. Vandalism, car-tyre slashing, thieving and *le racket* (pupils demanding money or envied items of clothing from others) were common. A twelve-year-old girl was sexually attacked by several older boys. A seventeen-year-old was hit and reportedly raped in the school toilets.

GANGING UP IN PRISON

Three teenagers jailed for the savage beating of a fellow pupil they had persistently bullied found themselves on the receiving end of similar treatment when they arrived at a remand centre to start three-year sentences for grievous bodily harm. When fellow prisoners read about the attack in which the victim almost died from internal bleeding, they greeted the perpetrators on their arrival with some violent treatment of their own. Recent research has revealed that a third of young offenders in custody aged sixteen to twenty-one said they had been bullied in the previous month; one in five was bullied with varying degrees of regularity and one in twenty was both a bully and a victim.

HELP AT HAND

The Arches is a club in South London where around a hundred teenagers, the members of five opposing gangs, gather each evening to make friends, music and cakes. The club's organiser, Camila Batmanghelidjh, thinks that gang membership appeals to these teenagers as a 'substitute family' and as a need 'to know there's a group of people looking out for them'. At first there were some ugly incidents at The Arches but now there is no gang hostility on site. The club has become a place that its teenage members have come to enjoy and trust, a place where they have no need to be defensive or aggressive and where they will find consistent care from adults. Staff members, a mixture of local people and about thirty counsellors, offer practical help as well as counselling.

Fourteen-year-old club member Natasha explains, 'This place is different, too extraordinary. They're like your parents and your friends. They don't try to embarrass you. They ask you questions like your parents would - what lessons did you have today, what did you eat? It's nice to be asked how was your day. And they appreciate every little thing you do here, no matter how little or how big.'

HOW SHOULD SCHOOLS DEAL WITH BULLYING?

Almost all children are bullied at some point in their school career.

A school is a community where a great many people come together over a period of years, during which time many of them are developing and changing. If bullying is to be avoided the school needs to create a climate of trust and to teach appropriate social behaviour. Bullying occurs when appropriate social behaviour has either not been established or when it has broken down.

Schools also have a responsibility to put in place strategies (not just policing) to ensure, as far as possible, that opportunities to bully are not available.

The school can also help both bullies and the bullied to modify their behaviour, and to find happier, more confident ways of getting on with others. Research studies have shown that schools can play a role in influencing troubled student behaviour even when this behaviour has resulted from family or community problems outside the school environment.

AN ANTI-BULLYING POLICY

If bullying is to be tackled, a school needs to have an anti-bullying policy rather than leave individual teachers to deal with each incident in isolation. Such a policy will be most effective if it is drawn up with input from everyone involved - the school governors, the students, the teachers, the playground supervisors, the dinner ladies, the caretaker and so on. In this way it can be tailor-made, taking into account a particular school's architecture, location and trouble spots; in addition everyone who works or studies there can be involved in monitoring and tackling bullying.

Of course, an anti-bullying policy cannot guarantee that bullying will never take place again. The school needs to monitor and check that its anti-bullying policy is still being implemented and still effective. And of course each year will bring new students and members of staff who will need to be involved in the policy's anti-bullying strategies.

Students need to be involved in shaping their school's anti-bullying policy.

A BLUEPRINT

These are some of the strategies that schools may adopt to help tackle or prevent bullying.

1. The whole school should be organised so that everyone who studies or works there is involved in monitoring and tackling bullying.

2. Everyone should be made aware that bullying is not allowed in the school in any form. A statement to this effect should be drawn up and given to every student and their parents. The statement should emphasise the positive role that everyone can play in encouraging caring and responsible attitudes to other people.

3. Students and staff should discuss the layout of the school and its grounds and the routes taken by pupils to and from school. They should identify where bullying takes place (for example, the corridors, the toilets, the school bus, the showers and so on) and at what time of day. These areas should be supervised.

4. Staff should avoid leaving classes unsupervised.

5. Students and staff should identify which groups of people are most likely to be bullied (for example: new first years, people who have transferred from other schools, student teachers, gay students, ethnic minority students, students with disabilities) and see whether there are ways they can be helped to feel safe. Older students, for example, could be given the responsibility of looking after new first years as they settle in.

6. Maps, notices and signs should be prepared so that new pupils can find their way round easily.

7. Students and teachers should organise workshops on bullying and issues connected with bullying, such as the acceptance of difference. This might include role plays and discussions. Parents might also be involved in these discussion groups.

8. Students should be encouraged to report bullying so that incidents can be discussed openly and constructively. Schools that use this approach report that joint discussions and analysis enable students to understand each other's viewpoints better and to reach a high level of deliberation and moral judgement. Some schools have regular children's courts at which bullying problems are aired. Parents should also be encouraged to contact the school if they believe their child is being bullied.

TELLING TALES?

9. Teachers should ensure that even in large schools, every student is very well known by at least one teacher who takes a special interest in her/him as an individual.

10. School rules should be clear and explicit and enforced by all the staff. Disciplinary procedures should be fair and consistently applied rather than harsh and punitive. In this way bullying students are offered an alternative model to their own aggressive behaviour. In addition, the idea that 'might is right' is replaced by more humane and understanding possibilities.

Question

Can you put these strategies in order of importance? Do others agree with your order?

> 66 **Intervention is hindered because there is a fine divide between 'telling' and 'grassing' and between 'just joking' and 'bullying'** 99
> A 1997 Keele University Report, *Anti-Bullying in Action*

One of the problems to do with reporting bullying in school is that there is a stigma attached in our society to what is called 'telling tales'. This means that the victims or witnesses of bullying are sometimes inhibited from reporting or complaining about bullying for fear of being called a 'grass', a 'telltale', a 'crybaby' or a 'wimp'. This unwritten code is obviously highly convenient for bullies.

In fact there is nothing dishonourable or humiliating about telling a teacher or parent about bullying. Bullying is frequently so vicious or so violent or so upsetting that it is not something that young people can deal with on their own without adult intervention. Enough is now known about the nature of bullying and its impact for most teachers and other adults to deal with the problem in a sensible and sensitive way. In a study of calls to a bullying helpline it was found that nearly three quarters of the children who had asked for adult help found that it had positive effects.

Sometimes, of course, teachers or parents do exacerbate the problem:

When Jane's headteacher talked to the school assembly about bullying, she did it in such a way that it was obvious to the bullies that Jane had 'told'. From then on, her life was a misery.

When Ravi's dad heard that his football kit had been torn and thrown around in the changing room, he went straight round to the school and made a scene. Ravi was jeered at for the rest of the term.

SCHOOL INITIATIVES

Schools are responding to the problem of bullying with a variety of strategies. Here are some examples:

Relationships campaign

A comprehensive school in Barrow-in-Furness started a 'relationships campaign' when the school's prefects were replaced by an elected council of senior pupils. Council members became aware of one pupil who was continually truanting. Chatting to him after school hours, they learnt that he was truanting because he was being bullied. They told staff, the matter was resolved and the truanting stopped. The school went on, with input from the school council and the governors, to devise a whole-school equal opportunities policy which is given a high profile so that 'everyone understands where the school community stands with regard to behaviour towards one another'. One initiative is that council members "adopt" a lower school form, meeting new pupils at their induction day in July and greeting them on their first day of term. 'A real bond is built up between council members, their adopted pupils and form tutors'. Council members also have counselling training, where they role-play, learn about different types of behaviour, the importance of listening to all sides of a story and of compromise. As a result, council members are often able to resolve conflicts themselves - although staff are always kept informed of what is going on.

Security cameras

At a comprehensive school in Solihull, security cameras were installed as a crime prevention measure after a spate of thefts occurred while the school was open for night classes and community activities. Two were positioned to cover the main entrances, one looked out over the playground and one surveyed the changing room corridor. However, as the cameras were recording 24 hours a day, the maintenance staff soon discovered that they were picking up incidences of bullying on tape. "You'd get pushing and shoving, maybe with three or four kids on to one youngster...or in the playground you'd spot a lump of kids gathering and you would want to know what was going on...they sometimes stand there waiting outside the back door for someone they want to get." The teachers realised that the recordings could be used in a positive way to get pupils to examine their behaviour. They now see the cameras as a useful tool in their programme against bullying.

Bully courts

Kidscape, the school anti-bullying programme, suggests the setting up of bully courts in school. Once a week, at an appointed time, the court - consisting of two children elected by the student body and two appointed by teachers, along with one teacher - meets to discuss and deal with incidents of aggressive behaviour. The court's verdict is filed and distributed to all those involved in the case; defendants have the right of appeal but are bound by the solutions or penalties of the court. Michele Elliott of Kidscape stresses that bully courts "can only work in schools which have established a caring atmosphere and in which the school contract is firmly in place." They should focus on bringing justice to bear on a person who has broken the rules, rather than seeking severe punishment.

The No Blame approach

The No Blame approach used in some schools is an attempt to change the group dynamics within a school. It mobilises the goodwill of the many nice young people who only observe or even join in bullying because they are under group pressure to conform. No Blame helps such people not to collude - they no longer join in bullying and they do not allow bullies to continue to behave in this way. The No Blame approach believes that while chat does not change bullies, neither will punishment. Punishment often makes things worse and victims often suffer revenge attacks after the punishment of bullies.

Space to talk things through

A school in London has two counsellors on-site. The aim is to provide emotional first aid to troubled pupils and reduce the strain on teachers. The counsellors offer individual counselling and group sessions on bullying. 17-year-old Michael has had counselling for the last year:

Question

"Chat does not change bullies, but neither will punishment." Do you agree?

Bullying troublespots

A survey of bullying troublespots was carried out by a school in Leeds, in 1996. It identified areas such as the girls' toilets where gangs tended to gather, a concrete ramp between the playground and the second floor (children feared being pushed off, or spat on while walking underneath), hidden corners where bullies can hide and a layout which offered bullies a variety of escape routes. Pupils also suggested appointing an anti-bullying worker to operate in the school and the surrounding community, an overhaul of the playground and posters and leaflets in school telling them who to approach about bullying.

> **"** My form tutor referred me. I've got this temper and I can't really handle it. I threw a chair across the room and hit a teacher in the face. I didn't want to go. I thought, 'I ain't a madman, I don't need counselling'. Then I beat up someone else...I decided to see what the counselling was like, just once. It was like telling a stranger all your business. When I went in I felt down. But when I came out, I felt high. It helped me a bit. In the last year I ignored anyone who started on me. I wouldn't fight back. I was lucky I hung on. They used to say I was the worst behaved person in the whole school. By the end, no one knew I was there. **"**

Buddies

At a mixed comprehensive in Bath, 14-year-old volunteers act as "buddies" to new pupils in a scheme funded by a grant from the charity Human Scale Education. All the volunteers undergo training in learning how to listen, respond to and empathise with disorientated young pupils. Their brief is not to solve serious problems but to share ideas, exchange views and express thoughts and feelings with a view to raising self-esteem.

Culture of Trust

An Office for Standards in Education report cited a Roman Catholic primary school in Nottingham as a place where no evidence of bullying was found. The school places emphasis on building trust by acknowledging not just academic success but also kindnesses, the importance of collaborative work and of respecting each other. The headteacher thinks the ethos of spiritual and moral values that pervades the whole school accounts for the absence of bullying.

Whatever schools wish to call it, this 'culture of trust' is what anti-bullying strategies should aim to create if they are to be truly effective.

GP IGNORED

"I have a number of young patients whom I know to be suffering from bullying at school, and am treating them accordingly, but while I am doing so, the situation remains unchanged at the school...Although I cannot give the names of the children involved, I have contacted the headteacher of one school, telling him of my concerns and offering to help, but there has been no response whatsoever, not even an acknowledgement."

Letter from Dr Peter Kandela to the *Times Educational Supplement*, July 1996

LOCAL COMMUNITY LINKS

In a study of a large secondary school in east London, researchers found that fifty-two per cent of students had been assaulted in the preceding year. Almost two thirds of the most serious incidents occurred within a quarter of a mile of the school, during the lunch breaks or at the end of the school day. Seventy-two per cent of the respondents knew the perpetrators of the violence against them and researchers concluded that in certain areas, schools are becoming the focus of neighbourhood conflict. In the neighbourhood in question, growing numbers of unemployed young people with few family or friendship links were becoming increasingly involved in local conflicts and loyalties.

> " Shopkeepers in Scarborough have launched a 'Safe Routes to School' scheme, based on a similar initiative in Australia. Shops in the scheme offer a safe haven to primary school children who feel threatened by bullying on their way to and from school. "

In a comparative study with a secondary school in a similar neighbourhood in the northwest of Paris, the researchers found that links were being built with the local community and pupils encouraged to talk about violence and crime. The French pupils run a community radio station from two classrooms producing chat shows and phone-ins dealing with these issues. The school also has a mentoring scheme that enables older school-leavers to work in the school during lunch breaks and immediately after school with younger pupils. Over the past ten years the neighbourhood has moved from having one of the highest crime rates in France to being just below the national average. The researchers conclude that initiatives are needed in Britain to bring teachers, youth workers, youth justice workers and police closer together in order to build a pupil-centred culture of safety.

STRATEGIES TO KEEP SAFE

If you are being bullied you need to take sensible precautions to avoid the bullies and you need to think about why you are being bullied so that you can build up your confidence in the right way for you:

1. Stick with your friends whenever you can. Be part of a group.

2. Keep within sight of a teacher or supervisor.

3. Try not to react to bullying by showing that you are upset or angry. Bullies lose interest in bullying people who don't react. (But don't blame yourself if you can't manage this. It is hard!)

4. Don't show off by wearing expensive clothes or jewellery to school or taking other expensive items with you.

5. Be aware of your behaviour - do you, for example, irritate people by being a know-all or by barging into groups you'd like to be part of? You may need help with your friendship skills. The booklist at the back of this book may be helpful.

6. If bullies take your dinner money or steal something of yours, try not to get into a fight about it unless you are confident that you will win. It's not worth being beaten up for the price of a school dinner. Report what happened as soon as possible.

Continued on next page

7. Practise your replies to things you may be teased or bullied about so that you can give the impression that it doesn't bother you. You know you're just fine as you are.

8. Remember that not telling helps bullies to go on bullying. If you can, tell your parents. Tell a trusted teacher what is going on too.

9. Don't suffer bullying for a long time. If you want to try and prevent it yourself - fine. But if you don't manage, don't let it drag on. The longer bullying goes on, the harder it is to stop.

10. Even if you become a karate black belt, there is no guarantee that you will never be bullied again. However, learning to fight properly at a self defence or martial arts class will almost certainly help you to feel and look more confident and this will lessen your chances of being picked on.

11. If bullies are trying to blackmail you (make you do something or give them something by threatening to reveal something you want kept secret), the best way to deal with it is either to report what is happening or call their bluff. If you can, say: "Tell whoever you like! I don't care."

12. Try not to get into fights. Unfortunately bullies are usually rather good at fighting. If you can't run away, you might be able to:

• bluff your way out (for example, pretend your form tutor is on his way to find you).

• walk away without responding to the jeers and insults. If you can't be drawn into insulting the bully back, s/he may lose interest.

• if you sense it might work, stand up to the bully by saying something direct like "You may not like me, but I want you to know that I'm not going to let you bully me/take my things any more!" Bullies expect the people they bully to be afraid of them.

• talk your way out. If you're good at arguments or have a good sense of humour, you might even be able to joke your way out of a tight spot. A lot of comedians started using humour in the playground to avoid being picked on.

13. As a last resort and if your school can't or won't help to stop bullying, you may be able to change schools. Discuss this with your parents.

14. Remember, not only is bullying a frequent occurrence but victims of bullying almost invariably need help and support to stop it. They also need to time to recover and get their confidence back. It's OK to feel angry and upset about what happened.

STRATEGIES TO STOP BEING A BULLY

If you are a bully, it is possible and very rewarding to change your behaviour so that you will feel better about yourself and people will want to offer you real friendship and respect. Here are some ideas that may be helpful:

1. Observe how other people get on together without needing to bully and control each other. Are there ways of doing things that you can learn from?

2. Are you a bully because you are bullied at home? If so, you know how painful it is to be bullied. Think of all the happy ways you would like to be treated and start trying to treat yourself and others like that.

3. Why not put your physical energies and aggression into sport? It's OK to win there by beating people as long as you stick to the rules.

4. Is it the end of the world if someone disagrees with you or if you don't get your own way? Think about the idea that other people see things from their point of view just as you see it from yours. It's OK to disagree. Try to accept that not getting your own way all the time is an inevitable part of life that is sometimes disappointing but rarely catastrophic.

5. Why not be a leader but without trying to dominate and control other people? Perhaps joining Guides or Scouts or an outward bound course would develop your leadership skills in good ways. Some schools have a mentoring scheme which involves older students looking after and helping younger ones. Perhaps you would enjoy taking someone younger under your wing.

6. Think about the heroes you admire on television, or in films and books. Do they, like Rambo, settle arguments by punching and shooting "enemies"? If so, try to think of other heroes who win through using other kinds of strength.

7. What is it about the people you bully or jeer at that irritates you? You may not realise, for example, that the man with the disfigured face was burnt in a car crash or that Nadine is clumsy because she was born with a hip defect. Try not to be frightened of people who seem different to you or indeed, of the different bits inside you. Everyone is different, everyone is unique and special.

8. Do you enjoy bullying because you like showing off in front of an audience? You can get that kind of enjoyment from acting in the school play or being good at sport - and these activities don't hurt other people.

Continued on next page

9. Think about the sort of situations in which you start to bully people. Can you find ways to avoid them? Can you think of alternative, better ways of dealing with your anger and frustration?

10. Anger is a very useful emotion because it tells you what you don't like about something or how you would like to be treated. It can also be a very creative emotion because once you understand what makes you angry, you can begin to think of constructive ways to improve or change things.

11. Remember that people who bully can get help to stop behaving in this destructive and unhappy way. Of course it takes a lot of courage to admit to being a bully and to admit to yourself that you want to change. Ring the Helplines listed at the back of this book or try talking to a sympathetic teacher.

HELPLINES AND ORGANISATIONS

Advisory Centre for Education (ACE)
22 Highbury Grove
London N5 2DQ
Tel: 0171 354 8321
Advice on education and on anti-bullying in schools for parents, teachers and governors.

Anti-bullying Campaign
185 Tower Bridge Road
London SE1 2UF
Tel: 0171 378 1446
Helps parents work with schools to combat bullying.

Changing Faces
1 & 2 Junction Mews
London W2 1PN
Tel: 0171 706 4232
Help and advice for children and young people with facial disfigurements.

Childline
Helpline: 0800 1111
(free and open 24hrs)
Freepost 1111
(no stamp needed)
London N1 OBR
A confidential helpline for children and young people in trouble or in danger.

Very experienced at dealing with bullying. Because of the huge demand, it is often difficult to get through, but do keep trying. Children can also write to Childline.

Children First
(free and open 24hrs)
Helpline: 0131 337 8539
41 Polwarth Terrace
Edinburgh EH11 1NU
A confidential helpline for children in trouble or in danger in Scotland. Very experienced at dealing with bullying.

The Children's Legal Centre
University of Essex
Wivenhoe Park
Colchester CO4 3SQ
Tel: 01206 873820
Legal advice on every area to do with children's rights.

The Commission for Racial Equality (CRE)
Elliot House
10-12 Allington Street
London SW1E 5HE
Tel: 0171 828 7022
Advice on racial discrimination or attacks.

Kidscape
152 Buckingham Palace Road
London SW1W 9TR
Helpline for parents of children who are bullied:
Tel: 0171 730 3300
(10-4 Mon-Fri)
A major centre for advice, training and publications about bullying.

Lesbian and Gay Switchboard
WC1N 3XX
Helpline: 0171 837 7324
24 hour counselling for lesbian and gay people

NSPPC (National Society for the Prevention of Cruelty to Children)
42 Curtain Road
London EC2A 3NH
Helpline: 0800 800500
(free and open 24hrs)
A confidential helpline for children in danger. Very experienced at dealing with bullying.

Quindo

2 West Heath Drive
London NW11 7QH
Tel: 0181 455 8698
Confidence building and
anti-bullying fitness
programme.

The Samaritans

Head Office
The Grove
Slough SL1 1QP
You will find the number of
your local branch in the
local phone directory or you
can ask the operator to put
you through. The Samaritans
offer confidential telephone
support, 24 hrs a day, to
despairing or suicidal people.

Young Minds

2nd Floor
102-108 Clerkenwell Road
London EC1V 2NP
Parents' Information Service:
0345 626376
Promotes the mental health
of children, young people
and their families.

IN AUSTRALIA
Department of Human Services

2 Lonsdale Street
Melbourne Vic 3000
Tel: (03) 9285 8888

Australian Drug Foundation

409 King Street
Melbourne Vic 3000
Tel: (03) 9328 3111

FURTHER READING

The following books are a small selection of recommended non-fiction titles. They should be available from your local library or can be ordered from good bookshops. You could try to get them ordered for your school library. There are also a large number of novels with bullying as a theme to look out for - such as Michael Coleman's *Weirdo's War* (Orchard), Jan Needle's *The Bully* (Hamish Hamilton) and Elizabeth Laird's *Secret Friends* (Hodder Children's Books).

For school students:
Elliott, Michele
The Wise Guide to Bullying
Hodder Children's Books

Naik, Anita
Friends or Enemies? The Ultimate Guide to Making Good Friends and Keeping Them
Hodder Children's Books

Stones, Rosemary
Don't Pick on Me: How to Handle Bullying
Piccadilly Press

For teachers and parents:
Besag, Valerie
Bullies and Victims in Schools
Open University Press

Childline
Children and Racism: A Childline Study
Childline

Elliott, Michele (ed)
Bullying: A Practical Guide to Coping for Schools
Longman

Elliott, Michele
101 Ways to Deal with Bullying: A Guide for Parents
Hodder & Stoughton

Lindenfield, Gael
Confident Children: Helping Children Feel Good About Themselves
Thorsons

MacLeod, Mary & Morris, Sally
Why Me? Children Talk to Childline about Bullying
Childline

Munro, Sheila
Overcome Bullying for Parents
Piccadilly Press

Pitts, John and Smith, Philip
Preventing School Bullying
Home Office Police Department

Index